The 30-Day Journey
From Prison to Spiritual Peace

Alicia thank you for your support. As you write allow God to lead you and be ready for the results.

THE
30-DAY JOURNEY FROM
PRISON
TO
SPIRITUAL PEACE

Josh Proby

REDHAWK
PUBLICATIONS

2019

Copyright 2019 by Joshua Proby

All rights reserved. No part of this publication may be reproduced, distributed, or transmitted in any form or by any means, including photocopying, recording, or other electronic or mechanical methods, without the prior written permission of the publisher, except in the case of brief quotations embodied in critical reviews and certain other noncommercial uses permitted by copyright law. For permission requests, write to the publisher, addressed "Attention: Permissions Coordinator," at the address below.

Redhawk Publishing is committed to publishing works of quality and integrity. In that spirit, we are proud to offer this book to our readers; however, the story, the experiences, and the words are the author's alone and Redhawk Publishing and its employees, subsidiaries, and controlling interests do not necessarily agree with the thoughts and conclusions drawn by the author.

ISBN: 9781794620810

Redhawk Publications
2550 Hwy 70 SE
Hickory , NC 28602

Transcribed from Mr. Proby's hand-written material and edited by Elizabeth Sagasar.

Edited by Rae Jenkins and Robert Canipe
rcanipe@cvcc.edu

Cover Photo and Author Photo by Janella Thaxton

Cover designed by Cheyenne Chumley
Concept by Rae Jenkins and Josh Proby
Execution by Clayton Joe Young and Robert Canipe
Thanks to Jonathan Lail for the graphic art suggestions!

Introduction

My life has been full of ups and downs, highs and lows. Pain plagued my life for many years, until I was placed in a prison, where I could not run anymore.

You may hear the word prison and ask, "What did he do to deserve that?" That question is one that deserves an answer: first-degree burglary.

So the next question is, "Why?" Because all my life things were taken from me. My sisters and brother were taken due to addiction. My innocence was taken when I was molested at age eleven. My sense of safety was taken by mental and emotional abuse.

Life taught to take, because that is all anyone did to me. The pain of my childhood led me to serve twelve years in prison, but rather than take away my freedom, incarceration ultimately led me to find freedom within. Each vignette in this book is a building block, part of a new foundation of understanding as well as a hammer to break down the internal prison that held me back long before I was behind actual bars.

Maybe, as you read this you are saying to yourself, "I've never been to prison. Why should Joshua's story matter to me?" So many of us live behind prison walls, whether we've ever been behind bars or not. Shame, fear, guilt, anger, frustration, distrust, addiction, abuse…The circumstances of our lives can cause us to build prison walls brick-by-brick, but we don't have to spend the rest of our lives behind prison walls of our own making.

So lets take a journey down the road of my life, so through it, you may find a deeper understanding of you, so you too can go from prison — to peace.

TABLE OF CONTENTS

CHAPTER 1: SPIRIT   11

Day 1   Stop Talking and Testify 13
Day 2   If You Don't Release Burdens You Will Become One 17
Day 3   There is Peace in Prayer 21
Day 4   Seeing Past Religion 25
Day 5   Having a Committed Spirit 29

CHAPTER 2: FAMILY   33

Day 6   Remember to Appreciate What You Have 35
Day 7   A Better You Makes a Family Complete 37
Day 8   A Family That Prays Together Stays Together 41
Day 9   Family 43
Day 10   A Child's Silent Cry 45

CHAPTER 3: LIFE   49

Day 11   Transition is the Proper Position 51
Day 12   Life 55
Day 13   It's Not the Moment, but the Opportunity 59
Day 14   Proper Perspective 63
Day 15   Sound the Alarm 65

CHAPTER 4: FRIENDSHIPS AND RELATIONSHIPS   71

Day 16   Egos: Relationships and True Relationships 73
Day 17   The Confusion of a Union 77
Day 18   Reputation Can't Be Built on What You're Going to Do 81
Day 19   Friendship 85
Day 20   Relationship 89

CHAPTER 5: RESPECT 93

- Day 21 Fair Gain 95
- Day 22 Respecting the Not So Obvious 99
- Day 23 It Is Not Who You Know, But Who Knows You 103
- Day 24 Respect Is Yours 107
- Day 25 Living Respect 111

CHAPTER 6: TIME 117

- Day 26 Silent Breath 119
- Day 27 Let Go When Time Expires 123
- Day 28 The Essence of Time 127
- Day 29 The Elimination of Time 131
- Day 30 Losing Track of Time 135

ABOUT JOSHUA PROBY 139

ACKNOWLEDGMENTS 141

An Introduction to Chapter 1

Although I was raised in the church, there were so many things going on outside of church that made me question if the spirit that lay within me was even alive.

I was mentally, emotionally, and physically abused, to the point that I would sit in the pews at church and go to sleep — not because I wasn't interested in the message, but because the pain I felt left my spirit empty.

The day that I was molested was the day I felt my spirit had left me; going forward in life I was merely existing, not truly living.

As I penned these words, I sat in a prison cell alone, not able to blame anyone; but I had the opportunity to look in the mirror and look at myself...and it was then that I was able to face all the pain.

Despite all of the hurt, I saw that the spirit I thought had left me was waiting for me to uncover it.

CHAPTER

ONE

SPIRIT

CHAPTER 1 :: DAY 1
Stop Talking and Testify

Many of us do a lot of talking, whether in person or on social media, but how often do we use our voices to testify about the goodness of the Lord?

When it comes to talking, people get into the habit of going on and on, carrying on conversations that have no true meaning, and no real value. How often when speaking to a friend, family member, or spouse, can testimony be heard in our conversation?

Every believer, regardless of background, has a testimony God can use to change the outlook of life for another. Sometimes when we speak, we seek to reinforce our own logic, or gain attention for ourselves. When we give control to the Holy Spirit, inviting God to use our words, our stories, our voices, He can use us for good. When our goal is dominating the conversation, or talking to pass time, the spirit has no room to influence the conversation.

Some people crawl into a shell when the spiritual things of life come up, but 2 Timothy 1:8 says, "So do not be ashamed of the testimony about our Lord or of me his prisoner. Rather, join with me in suffering for the gospel, by the power of God." Sometimes we just want to chat about sports or the weather, and not every conversation is a Jesus-conversation, but Christ should be seen in and through what we say. The more we allow our conversations to be led by the Spirit, the more our conversations will be saturated with substance, rather than being engulfed in daily problems and complaints.

For the Spirit to have full reign in our lives, we must be bold in our testimony; our boldness must be in what God has delivered us from. God delivered me from a twelve-year incarceration and because of my testimony, when I speak — I speak of the joy, the love, and the wisdom I gained. By honoring God more than my past condition, the Spirit can flow, and bless those who I come in contact with.

What has God delivered you from? The Lord may have delivered you from drugs, past pain, smoking, abuse — whatever He has freed us from, we honor Him best when we focus on His mercy, and not the logic of this world.

Why is the natural human drive to speak so strongly ingrained in most of us? Maybe because listening takes patience and time, while frivolous talking allows us to hide from the fear of rejection or judgment, and to avoid true intimacy by complaining instead of embracing someone else's truth with a closed mouth and two open ears. Maybe we don't fear the testimony — we fear the truth the Spirit will reveal; a truth that displays our authentic selves in a light that may not initially be bright or appealing.

This state of truth, of living in the light, brings peace.
It is in this state that we can help others move beyond the superficial.

The mis-education of 'testimony' is that it can only be shared in a church. Truth is spoken each time we open our mouths to testify of the goodness of God, rather than make small talk in order to avoid real conversation.

Testimonies are not all about presentation, but obedience to the Spirit that allows the Spirit of God to be seen in you, and through all you do. Your testimony is your life, and your words provide the detail. God has allowed us to be where we are today for a reason and the things we have been through to get here are testimonies. Testimonies are followed by how you live your life.

Not every conversation we have should be serious — balance matters, and Jesus enjoys a hearty laugh just as we do; there is a productive balance that must be implemented. Our duty in life is to elevate each person we can to have a deeper relationship with Jesus.

ASK YOURSELF...

1. Are you allowing your talking to take you more into the world, and further from the flow of the Spirit?

2. What would it look like in action, if you focused more of your conversations on sharing your testimony, rather than idle chit-chat?

3. What percentage of your time in conversation is spent talking? What percentage of time do you spend listening? How would your conversations change, if you flipped those two numbers?

CHAPTER 1 :: DAY 2
If You Don't Release Burdens You Will Become One

The Bible speaks of two types of burdens: the Greek "baros," defined simply as 'a weight' — or anything pressing on one physically, and the second, "phortion" which is defined as 'something carried.' In life we must learn how to separate these two burdens in order to embrace the grace God offers us.

Unresolved fear, grief and other problems cause pain not just to ourselves, but to others as well. Individuals with unresolved problems are hindered emotionally, spiritually, even physically — and we are not capable of removing all the problems in our lives. Only God can do that.

When we try to conquer our burdens without the guidance of the Spirit, we become fragile. The things that weigh us down: addiction, illness, financial or marital struggles — become a baros weight, and we strive to rid ourselves of these burdens as quickly as possible.

When our lives are overwhelmed by baros weight, we cannot see how God can magnify Himself through our flaws; our eyes are focused more on what we see, and how far we are from getting better on our own, than on the power of God. We strive so hard to become self-reliant, bearing these baros burdens on our own, that we begin to be defined by our struggles. The burdens we cling to weigh down our thinking, emotions, physical being — most importantly our spirit, and we begin to blame others for our problems, losing trust in everyone, even God. This baros burden becomes a self-destructive force, and suddenly you are your own worst enemy, far from the strong and capable person you believed yourself to be.

Stop for a moment and say this aloud: There is liberty in Christ!

Romans 8:18 says, "I consider that our present sufferings are not worth comparing with the glory that will be revealed in us."

God does not intend for our burdens to rule over us. He reminds us in Matthew 11:30, "For my yoke is easy and my burden is light." This is the burden of phortion: anything God places on us is light, because we don't have to carry it — Christ carries it for us.

That does not mean we won't face difficult situations, but God promises as long as we face challenges in spirit and truth, He will give us the strength to overcome. 'Phortion' burdens are gifts wrapped in unpleasant situations, arriving in torn packages; the blessing lies in choosing what type of burden you will face.

Maybe we've lost a loved one, or lost a job. Maybe financial setbacks are dragging us down, or we are held hostage by addiction. In the midst of these trials, we can choose which burden we will make it. We can become engulfed in the pain and allow this baros burden to cloud our spiritual vision. Or — we can accept this challenge as a phortion burden; the circumstances are hard, unpleasant, maybe even impossible-seeming, but when we place our trust in God, He will show us what He wants us to do from that point, and He will carry the weight, and renew your spirit.

"'For I know the plans I have for you,' declares the Lord, 'plans to prosper you and not to harm you, plans to give you hope and a future.'"
— Jeremiah 29:11

The burdens of God are meant to define us — not deny us. As trials arise in life, we should ask ourselves, "Am I becoming a burden to myself and others, or am I overcoming a burden and helping others do the same?" Denial only blocks God, and prohibits the flow of the Spirit in our lives.

Every position God places us in is for victory — not defeat. When we allow ourselves to be comfortable in a position of defeat, everything outside of that place seems complicated — but this is not what God intends for us. Why stay defeated, when we can live in peace?

God is our strength when we are weak. 2 Corinthians 12:9 says, "But he said to me, 'My grace is sufficient for you, for my power is made perfect in weakness.' Therefore I will boast all the more gladly about my weaknesses, so that Christ's power may rest on me."

The burdens of this life can only make us stronger — as long as our burdens are tied to Jesus, and not our own abilities. God will give us strength and carry our burdens for us, when we choose to hand them to Him and trust Him to bear the weight.

ASK YOURSELF...

1. What burdens are you carrying right now?

2. How does this weight on your shoulders affect you? How does it impact the lives of those around you?

3. Have you given these burdens to God, or are you trying to carry them alone?

4. When is the last time you surrendered completely to Jesus, trusting Him to handle the tough situations in your life?

CHAPTER 1 :: DAY 3
There is Peace in Prayer

Certain things in life bring out the best in us…or the worst in us. To maintain balance, we turn to so many earthly things — but these things don't establish true balance, they only numb the pain. Power. Money. Material bliss. Sex. All these things serve as temporary escapism to help us avoid facing the truth.

So what can help? Prayer.

Philippians 4:6 encourages us to reach out to God in prayer, "Do not be anxious about anything, but in every situation, by prayer and petition, with thanksgiving, present your requests to God."

Sometimes prayer gets a bad rap. Even among believers, there are individuals more concerned with what they can get out of prayer — and if they don't get what they want, they tend to discredit the power of prayer. For years, I was one of those people. Despite growing up in the church, I found myself turning to prayer in certain situations, only to get what I expected to get. After many failed attempts of asking and not getting, I read the passage above and took a new approach. I realized I needed to dedicate my prayer life to God, and commit my heart to pleasing Him, rather than seeking selfish ends.

God answers prayers that come from a place of surrender, inviting the truth, and the Spirit of God to flow in and through that truth. The expectation of prayer should be placed not on the external — but on internal richness.

Psalms 62:5 says, "Yes, my soul, find rest in God; my hope comes from him."

Anything that happens in our lives has potential to blossom — or become corrupted — based on our personal relationship with God, established through prayer. There is no relationship, friendship, or marriage that I know that can remain strong without studying each other, and without communication. So our relationship with God cannot be strong without studying His word, the Bible, and praying to our Father.

Prayer brings peace, when our hearts are set on God and we allow the Spirit to lead us in the path of righteousness. We cannot convince God of the merit of our selfish desires through prayer or otherwise. It is a joy to let go of our egotistical reasoning, to set aside pride and vanity, and to ask God to move and work in our lives on His timeline, and according to His good plan.

Prayer is a place where we can lay down all that has been keeping us from being the child of God that Jesus died for. We can bring it all to Him in prayer with a heart turned toward pleasing God — not ourselves. Prayer is the communication line that allows the Spirit of God to make requests for us, so we can let God in and let Him save us from ourselves.

Through prayer, God can reveal what we need to build a more godly character. When we discredit prayer, we are denying God the open and loving communication He wants with us, and turning to prayer only in times of crisis causes us to lose out on so much of what God has to offer. But even then — God is gracious enough to allow us to feel the peace of prayer — even when we're stuck in our messes; He wants us to see that His peace is more powerful and more important than all our selfish wants.

Stop. Think. Erase all the things that are superficial. Allow the Spirit of God to awaken you through daily prayer that erases *you* and focuses on God. It is not what prayer can get you physically, but what God can make of you spiritually.

ASK YOURSELF...

1. When is the last time you prayed?

2. Do you consider yourself a faithful Prayer Warrior, or more of a Prayer EMT (Emergency Management Technician)?

3. Are you willing to surrender all to God?

4. If you've fallen out of the habit of prayer, or have been focused on self-serving prayer, it can be helpful to add regular prayer-sessions to your schedule. What time of day can you add prayer to your to-do list? Set a reminder on your phone, or write it into your daily agenda.

CHAPTER 1 :: DAY 4
Seeing Past Religion

When people look at you, do they see religion, or do they see Christ in you?

There are many religions in the world, each with a unique set of rules to follow. Many of them believe in God, and His good plan for all of His children. One thing Christians have in common, no matter which spiritual tradition we follow, is that others often see evidence of our religious preferences before they experience the love of God through us.

Each religion does not coincide perfectly with the other, which brings about division; this is exactly what the enemy wants.

John 10:10 says, "The thief comes not but to steal, and to kill, and destroy."

Too often, we let the ways of man cloud our spiritual sense, and begin to side with man.

Even in the Word of God, Jesus never stopped trying to instruct, and tell the truth to the religious leaders, the Pharisees. Even unto death, Jesus said, "Forgive them Father, for they know not what they do." [Luke 23:24]

Each religion knows that God is not of division. Amos 3:3 states, "Can two walk together, accept they both agree?" God does not want division — He wants unity; but man has used his own intellect to sway the people, which leads to a double mind which James 1:8 says, "Leaves one unstable in all ways."

We as people, as followers of Christ, have become unstable when it comes to religion.

The more people stand on religion, and not on the Word of God, the more we hinder and harm the building of the Kingdom of God. Individuals begin to despise one another based on man's view and not what the Word of God says.

People will actually disassociate themselves from one another based on what religion says, but religion is not God. Many become so engulfed in religion they miss the purpose of faith in God, which is bringing people to the knowledge of Christ.

I am not saying we should keep coming back to a person who openly denounces Christ, but too often people close the door before anything can be shared, based not on God's will, but on their personal religious convictions.

We should ask ourselves, if God looked upon us through our own narrow lens, how many of us would fall short? I am not trying to change anyone's religious convictions, but what I am doing is standing on the foundation of Jesus Christ, and remaining open to people of any religion who want to hear about the goodness of Christ. I also want to love those who reject Him, as I believe Jesus wants us to do.

Romans 12:1 says, "Therefore, I urge you, brothers and sisters, in view of God's mercy, to offer your bodies as a living sacrifice, holy and pleasing to God—this is your true and proper worship."

Our duties as believers in Christ is to throw down religion and pick up Christ. During my incarceration of twelve years, there were many who did not share my belief in Jesus Christ. This did not stop me from being friends with them. If our goal is to be an effective witness for Christ, we will learn the art of finding common ground, and opening doors so the spirit of God can flow through us in a way that helps the other person see and hear Christ in us. I played ball and worked out with people of differing beliefs, and opportunities like this gave my fellow inmates the chance to learn what I stood for was real, and it made them want to know more about Jesus.

Religion is man-made, and meant to divide us. We cannot let the enemy win, because Christ in us is greater than anything the world can throw at us. Peace. Love. Humility. Kindness. All are associated with God, and have nothing to do with religion. We must not neglect these fruits of the Spirit, or neglect offering them to everyone we encounter, including those who do not believe in Jesus. It is up to us to embody Christ so others can see Him through us.

The Jesus challenge for your life (not just today) is to show all the power of Jesus not just in what you say, but in how you act. How you respond to others, how open you are to listening, not just preaching — answering this challenge on a daily basis will bring you closer to others, and closer to God's will.

Religion is not the judge — God is. The Spirit of God is our comforter, and as we follow His Spirit, we will be comforted, and just as Jesus did, we will be able to reach out in Christian love to comfort others.

Let's begin a life that seeks Christ in everyone we meet, no matter their current state, and leave religion on the shelf when it comes to sharing Jesus.

ASK YOURSELF...

1. Are you allowing your talking to take you more into the world, and further from the flow of the Spirit?

2. What would it look like in action, if you focused more of your conversations on sharing your testimony, rather than idle chit chat?

3. What percentage of your time in conversation is spent talking? What percentage of time do you spend listening? How would your conversations changed if you flipped those two numbers?

CHAPTER 1 :: DAY 5
Having a Committed Spirit

Many of us struggle with the concept of commitment. Having a spirit that is committed serves as an even higher challenge, seeing that a physical commitment to anything is already a struggle.

Matthew 26:41 says, "Watch and pray so that you will not fall into temptation. The spirit is willing, but the flesh is weak." This verse shows us that the spirit is willing to commit, while the flesh fights against it. For many years, the only things I committed to were things that pleased me from an external point of view. Galatians 5:22-23 discussed the Fruit of the Spirit — the aspects of character we must be committed to internally.

One reason we find spiritual commitment difficult is because we lack self-control. Instead of the control that strives for peace and bridles the tongue, the control that even when you know you're right is restrained to serve justice to spiritual understanding, we choose self. We defend our egos, putting our personal desires before our spiritual commitments.

The confusion begins when we love the chaotic things of this world, and try to make a spiritual commitment through the chaotic things in our life. To have a spirit that is committed, we must prepare our hearts to endure hardship, to be patient, to exercise greater self control, above and beyond our circumstances.

The justification that many of us tend to use lies in what we have allowed to become dominant in our lives, excuses ranging from taking care of the children, career pressure, or simple unwillingness to let go of self in exchange for giving control to Christ.

If we will but submit unto God, we will see exactly what God wants us to be. You can become the person you never thought you could be. The struggle, pain, and frustrations of life are merely stepping stones to your ultimate position in life. A spirit that is committed keeps you from conforming to the ways of your lower self; the ways of the world will always leave you empty. Without a commitment, we deny ourselves of the promises, by committing we receive life. What do you choose?

ASK YOURSELF...

1. What have you let go of in order to be more committed to Christ?

2. What are you still holding on to that might be a stumbling block in your desire to commit more fully to your faith?

3. Are you content to be an off-and-on believer?

4. What priorities could you change in your life that would allow you to put your spiritual commitment ahead of your physical needs and worldly interests?

An Introduction to Chapter 2

As I sat in a room, physically bound, but spiritually becoming free, I could not help but think about my family. My son, my daughter, and how much I missed them. But I also felt the pain of neglect from my family. In two years, I had only received one letter. I felt like I was buried alive, and I was yelling for help, but nobody heard me. I ached each night thinking my family had forgotten about me. In that moment, a voice in my head said, "As I am restoring you, your family is being restored as well." At the time I did not know if I was going crazy, or the walls were beginning to talk. When I woke up, all the anguish I felt toward my family was flipped; I viewed the pain as an opportunity to see my family in the light that I knew it could be, and I knew it would be a reality.

A few weeks later I got a letter: "Son, I love you." It was my mom. My heart rejoiced, my spirit felt alive, and my life began its transformation.

Are you ready to follow along on this journey with me? Let's go!

CHAPTER TWO

FAMILY

CHAPTER 2 :: DAY 6
Remember to Appreciate What You Have

"I can't stand my mother." "I can't stand my father." "I really don't like my sister because she always gets on my nerves." "My brother...he thinks he's better than me!"

Sometimes, in a moment of frustration, we say things like this without realizing the powerful effect of our words. Over time, negativity like this within a family can take on a life of its own, sometimes even making us feel as if our family is more of a hindrance than a help.

Every family faces challenges, and every family sometimes struggles. Whatever labels we might use to describe our family, dysfunctional or functional, irrational or rational, none of these terms will ever mean more than the word that comes after all of those descriptors, and that is family. A family is not meant to always be your friend, but to be your support system. A family will not always give you what you want, but should always strive to provide what you need — not just in a superficial aspect, but in a way that strengthens you emotionally, spiritually, and mentally, which in turn teaches you to deal with life respectfully.

We must step back to evaluate self and appreciate our family. As crazy as it may sound, there are many people who would give anything just to have a family — even with all the problems involved, because they have never had one. Yes there are many that came from a family like myself, where I was mentally/emotionally abused as well as physically abused. And the painful memories from that alone would naturally make anybody refrain from wanting family ever again. But if I take the pain from what I know was not right, continue to carry it and destroy the possibility of my building the opposite of what was presented to me, I rob myself of the peace, the love that a family can provide, due to my not facing the pain and letting it go.

I did that for years, and lost what family truly can provide. Broken members in a family due to lingering pain, can only present broken pieces to a family. So keep in mind it is not the family that is the problem, it is the brokenness within the individual that must be looked at. The more we become grateful for family, the more we recognize the worth of a family, the more we will appreciate our family despite the hardship families can face.

Regardless of how divided it may seem, we can never forget the value of a family. Love, forgiveness, persistence, loyalty, patience... when problems arise, don't just look at the problem — look at what the family needs to be centered on to succeed beyond current circumstances. In this we will learn to appreciate family not just in the good times, but in the bad as well.

ASK YOURSELF...

1. How do you show your family appreciation?

2. How do you respond to your family or an individual member of your family, when you don't get the response you are hoping for?

3. Do you ever miss family gatherings or events because you have allowed temporary challenges or problems to create separation?

4. How have you contributed to the level of frustration or dysfunction within your family?

5. What could you say or do to help your family become stronger?

CHAPTER 2 :: DAY 7
A Better You Makes a Family Complete

Many times in life, all types of family issues are thrown our way. Not all things can be prevented when it comes to the problems that rise up against a family — which is why it is so vital to appreciate your family, and to know whose family you're in connection with: the family of Christ.

Joshua 24:15 says, "But if serving the Lord seems undesirable to you, then choose for yourselves this day whom you will serve, whether the gods your ancestors served beyond the Euphrates, or the gods of the Amorites, in whose land you are living. But as for me and my household, we will serve the Lord." In order for our families to be strong, we have to take a stand. We have to be bold not just in discipline, not just in finances, not just in control, but bold in the Lord.

Whether you are the mother, a daughter, or a father — becoming better starts with you.

When we are bold for Christ, then we can stand on the most important thing: Christ and Christ alone, declaring that it is Christ whom we will serve in our home and in our lives. Families have been torn apart by the enemy using addiction, infidelity, irresponsibility, fear, anger, abuse, to destroy our families. But family is a unit, and if one area is off then the other areas tend to be off as well.

Joshua took a stand as the head of the house, and boldly said, "As far as me and my house, we will serve the Lord." This is a bold declaration. Many of our men today have women play roles they are not intended to play, which causes the house to be out of alignment.

Men must be stronger in the responsibility that comes with being leaders and providers for their family. Of course not everyone will get it right off the cuff, but it is each person's role in the house to stay in tune with God. A better you makes a better family. We model to our families the way we respond to the challenges in our lives so we must be attentive to our own behavior.

Growing up, I had a weak family structure: my mother was absent, I never knew my father, my sister and brothers were spread out, and I was abused. Not that great of a family structure, right? As I grew, I realized if I wanted better for my own family, it was going to start with me. Point-blank. Period.

One thing that was instilled in my household was the gospel of Jesus Christ. During this journey, there were many ups and downs dealing with the pain of the past; but if I only reflected on what was, I would give my memories more power than God in my family's life. So I took a stand as Joshua did. I was bold in Christ, and built a structure that as for me and my house — we will serve the Lord.

Rather than set my family up for disappointment, I stood on the foundation of Jesus Christ. I chose to serve my family through Him, and allowed them to see Christ in me. My family is better today not because I am great, but because I stood on Christ, lived in Christ, and showed my family it starts with me. They knew of my past. They knew the things I had been through, from being molested, to abuse, to being incarcerated. But it was not my failures they rested in, because I did not rest in them. They rested in my hope, my faith, and the power of God — because that is what I displayed.

My family is amazing today because despite my pain, I decided that as for me and my house — we will serve the Lord. I have asked God to use me to show my family love, regardless of what pain they have endured.

Are you ready to be better first for the Kingdom, so you can be better for your family?

A better family starts with you. The better we become as leaders, as Joshua was, the more complete we become as a family. If seen only through the natural eye, the imperfections of each member of a family can seem like a disaster — but if we keep the mind of Christ, we will see how God can blend us together to give other families hope.
Titles in the home are just that, until responsibility is attached to the title for meaning to come from it. Everyone must start with themselves, working to lighten the load for the next one in line,

functioning as a team and working toward a shared goal of following God. When we do that, "family" will have an even bigger impact in the world we live in today.

ASK YOURSELF...

1. What did "family" mean to you growing up?

2. How have your early family experiences shaped your family today?

3. Is God at the center of your family? What can you do to invite Him to be a greater part of your family?

4. Communication is key. Schedule face-to-face time (or on the phone, if far apart) to talk to members of your family about how much you value them, and share your commitment to following Christ, and being an example of His love to the ones you love most.

CHAPTER 2 :: DAY 8
A Family That Prays Together Stays Together

When we hear the word 'family' a lot of things come to mind, such as respect, proper morals, unity, love, and the list goes on. Not all families embody these qualities, because — let's be honest — family does not ring the same happy bell for every individual.

You may be asking yourself, "How can I have a successful family of my own, when what I call 'family' displays the opposite of ideal family qualities?" Before answering that question, you must allow your mind to be receptive to a suggestion that can help you find your answer. A family is unique; it is a whole, not a half, not a part — each person of the family plays a major role in the family success as a whole. Although everyone in the family presents his or her own challenges to one another, we must overcome despite our hardships, in order to make our families stronger. And this is something we cannot do alone — we need help.

This is where the power of prayer comes in. Prayer is not going to change a family overnight. Prayer is not going to stop people in your family from making mistakes. What prayer will do, in the midst of hardship, trial, and tribulation, is keep a family together. How is this possible? Prayer by a family willing to better themselves as individuals, and the family as a whole, gives knowledge, understanding, and patience in the midst of the growing pains your family experiences.

By the power of prayer, family becomes more than a bunch of people who come together and get on each other's last nerve. Each member, despite their character defects, begins to feel understood.

The family can begin to work together to heal individually, and as a group. This healing process allows a family to share props, listen to one another, and to come up with positive solutions to difficult situations — together.

As a family comes together to deal with their own personal issues it can seem like having a family is more of a curse than a blessing, but the truth still holds: A family that prays together, stays together. Prayer becomes the family's foundation, allowing the family to lean on each other, and on God. The prayer of a committed family supports the entire group.

James 5:16 says, "Therefore confess your sins to each other and pray for each other so that you may be healed. The prayer of a righteous person is powerful and effective."

Prayer does not erase or replace, prayer heals and teaches, and establishes new promises. Our communication with our Lord and Savior Jesus Christ is vital, although at times it may seem our prayers are not being heard. All of our prayers will be answered right on time.

So, don't give up on your family, and don't shy away from developing the principles needed to deeply root strong family qualities. Believe in your family, believe in yourself, and believe in the power of prayer.

ASK YOURSELF…

1. When is the last time your family joined in prayer together?

2. What stops you from praying together as a family? Is it awkward? Are there member(s) of your family who don't believe in the power of prayer? Have you simply fallen out of the habit?

3. How can you be a leader in your family, inviting other members to pray together, or for each other? Could you start a prayer chain? Could you implement prayer at family gatherings? Could you share in prayer on the phone, or in email, if your family lives apart from each other?

4. If calling all members of your family to prayer is challenging, what can you do to let them know you are praying regularly for your family as a group, and individually?

CHAPTER 2 :: DAY 9
Family

Family is a word that can be very dear to a person's heart, and in some cases can rip another's apart.

Although everyone may not have the best family in the world, it still should not change how a family should be viewed. The relationships we have within our family are based on our view of the importance of family. The individual who grows up in the best of circumstances is not exempt from viewing family in a negative way. The single parent home, the child that is promised things only to be let down, are also individuals who grow up to believe that family is not of great importance. With this type of pain lingering in one's mind, these same children grow up to have their own families, and due to poor teaching, often develop the same (whether good or bad) principles they were raised with — even when they despise those principles.

In the wake of this inheritance, family may never have a chance to be viewed in its proper form. How can a family be a family if they've never understood what a family really is? Yes, they may know the principles a family should have, and they may want the best for their family, but past pains hinder one from establishing a true family. This, of course, is not something that is done on purpose, but often unconsciously. Many of us understand what it takes to uphold the family, such as providing for a family's needs, and being present, but the biggest obstacle may be a lack of positive family experience. Early positive experiences with family teach us that a family bond is not about a 'me first attitude,' but that family is about holding each other up when one or more of us are down.

Wealth and position do not solidify a family; family is not about the tangible, but the intangible, which is more valuable than anything money can buy.

Despite our upbringing, we must realize that poor teaching cannot be accepted and passed on to our own families. We must strive to eradicate that frame of mind. How do we do that? By allowing ourselves to want better for another than what we may have experienced growing up.

Family is a bond that should not be broken. Family is a concept that must be modeled, not just a word to be spoken. The ingredients for positive family living are found not in the physical, but the internal. The choice to give our total selves, not in words but in actions, develops a strong bond that is much harder to break down.

Do not allow previous missteps to hinder your family. Build your family and as you grow, watch the strength of your family do the same.

ASK YOURSELF...

1. What was family life like for you, growing up?

2. How has your early experience with family shaped your attitude toward your own family today?

3. What do you observe in your family today, that is an echo of your upbringing — either positive or negative?

4. Fast forward ten, twenty, thirty or more years into the future, when your own children (or family) start families of their own. What legacy of family life do you want to pass on to them? Which aspects of family life would you want to stop them from carrying into the future?

CHAPTER 2 :: DAY 10
A Child's Silent Cry

This part was specifically meant for last, because every parent was a child, and every child has a voice. The voice of a parent needs to be heard, but the voice of a child is just as important.

Families are torn apart before they can even be shaped because the child that is now an adult did not have a voice. They go on to have children of their own, and never know how to allow their child to have a voice due to how they were raised.

Growing up, my voice was drowned out by an emphasis on structure and stringent expectations. Get good grades. Go to church. Say 'Yes sir,' and, 'Yes ma'am.' All of which are good, but in the midst of it, when I had a question, I was not allowed to ask. When I saw something that may not have been right, I had to stay in a child's place. The platform for conversation was not there, which led to an emotionally and mentally closed-off adult, and as a parent, I was teaching from my hurt — not from my love. I did not want my child to experience what I had, but unconsciously caused them to go through what I had wanted to prevent--maybe not physically, but mentally, emotionally, and spiritually.

Every family is made up of adults who were once children. Mark 10:15-16 says, "Truly I tell you, anyone who will not receive the kingdom of God like a little child will never enter it. And he took the children in his arms, placed his hands on them and blessed them."

The point Jesus makes is regardless of age, we must always remain teachable — as a child, always learning.

My favorite part is Jesus' response to those willing to receive His kingdom 'as a child': He put his hands upon them and blessed them. Jesus realized that the future is not in our parenting style alone, but in our children. Not just in being an adult, but in becoming like a child before God, so as we learn from God, our children can learn from us, and we can hear and respond with love when our children cry out.

The world we live in today tells us to check our social media followers more often than we ask how our child's day was at school. Then we wonder why they listen to the world more than they listen to parental instruction.

So, I pose this question: When is the last time you behaved as a child before God, asking to be guided and held in His arms? Children, when was the last time you found safety in God and your parents, over the false love of the world? As a family we can learn so much from one another. And as leaders of our family, our ears must be attentive to the silent cries of our children. Even as adults we must realize that God hears our silent cries, and allow God's ways to teach us to hear the silent cries of our own children, who will one day be the molders of another generation.

ASK YOURSELF...

1. Did you feel listened to, known, and loved as a child?

2. How do your childhood experiences of family contribute to who you are as a person now, either positively or negatively?

3. How has your family history shaped who you are as a parent (if you have children)? How has this history shaped the way you relate to your parents, siblings, or other family members today?

4. What would you change about your current family dynamics, if you could?

5. What steps could you take, beginning today, to implement positive change with your children, spouse, or other family members?

An Introduction to Chapter 3

Sitting in a room no bigger than a bathroom for two years of your life takes its toll. As my spirit was becoming renewed day by day, I still had the question in my mind, "How does all of this transition into everyday life?"

For years my life was filled with pain.

I sat in prison in 2010, and I would not be released until 2018. All of the pain I felt was caused by family had been faced; although my family was miles and miles away, I knew I had a chance, and most importantly I had hope. Being in such a negative environment with hope of change was dangerous in itself.

So, I had a choice: Wait to see what life had to offer until I got out, or begin to see the opportunity I had where I was. This is a choice we all have. Despite the prison we may be faced with, we must ask ourselves: Will we view life from only one side, or choose to see the many different ways life can take place? At that time, I was able to see a reality not many in my position could see.

As I lay alone at night, crying silent tears, life in my mind was very real. Each day I lived what I envisioned and refused to let my physical reality (life behind bars) dictate my emotional and spiritual reality. My spirit was becoming stronger; I began to embrace many important views of family — now I just had to fit it all into the grand scheme of life.

Are you still with me? Good — let's keep going.

CHAPTER THREE

LIFE

CHAPTER 3 :: DAY 11
Transition is the Proper Position

Transition is key, but how many people are willing to work through transition to bring about change?

Nothing happens overnight, but overnight is about how much patience we have for a change to take place. The focus is always on the change, but little attention is paid to what is needed along the journey. We are willing to change for the acceptance or the liking of another, but changes made to impress someone else don't always stick.

Change in life can be heavy, depending on a person's ability to accept failure and properly channel that energy. When we channel our failures into positive action, a transitional phase begins: thoughts become more mature, responsibility becomes an action instead of a reaction, and emotions become more than just a feeling. These are some key attributes that are essential for transition.

When change fails to take root, it is important to remember, that in life, people fail transition, transition does not fail us. This happens because the transition is more mature than the person who wants to change.

Romans 12:2 says, "Do not conform to the pattern of this world, but be transformed by the renewing of your mind. Then you will be able to test and approve what God's will is--his good, pleasing and perfect will."

Transition requires us to abandon what we think we know according to the world that has engulfed us and stagnated us, in order to become receptive to the promises God has for us. This is an obstacle greater than a mere hurdle; a hurdler can see the object ahead and prepare to avoid it, but we are not always aware of the obstacles put in place by our attitude or lack of knowledge.

Transition has phases we must complete in order to bring about a complete change in life. To be transformed we must be renewed in our mind and the renewing of a mind starts not with what's outside of you, but begins within you. Impatience, anger, stubbornness, selfishness, are aspects of a person's character that can bleed into our daily lives. These character attributes become obstacles because we refuse to accept the transition that is needed to erase those things that have stagnated our lives. We fall back on the age-old excuse, "This is just how I am," failing to complete a transition because we choose not to rise above our lesser inclinations.

This is not something God has placed in our lives, but something we have placed over the promises God has for us. How easily we accept the tendency to regress, rather than progress. When we trust regression rather than progress, we begin to project the hardships of life onto others. All the while, transition and the renewing of your mind wait patiently for you to surrender to change.

What is life to you? Who are you now, and who do you want to be? How much time and energy have you given over to positive transitions in your life?

We cannot manipulate the phases of transition if transformation is our goal. A conscious spiritual effort is vital to transition, while a mind that refuses understanding is paralyzed. Transition is the key to change in any walk of life, but we must embrace the phases of transition in order for real life change to happen.

Self is often our biggest stumbling block to change, but finding out who we are in Christ is when we discover life.

ASK YOURSELF...

1. What area(s) of your life feel stagnant, and ready for positive change and growth? Consider your work life, home life, and relationships.

2. Choose a single area of transition and outline the steps necessary to create positive change in this area.

3. How would your life improve once this particular transition is complete?

4. Are you willing to undertake Step 1 on your list? Why or why not?

5. Who is available to support you as you transition and transform?

CHAPTER 3 :: DAY 12
Life

When the word transition comes up, the Scripture verse that comes to mind is Ecclesiastes 7:10, "Do not say, 'Why were the old days better than these?' For it is not wise to ask such questions."

In our transition stage in life, we tend to kick against what God is trying to do in our lives. Transition is key, but how many people are willing to go through transition phases to bring about a change without looking back?

Nothing happens overnight, yet overnight is how we as people expect life and all its woes to change. The focus is always on the change, but little attention is paid to the transition that leads up to that change.

At times, we want change for all the wrong reasons. Acceptance from others, fear, low self-esteem, wanting change for these reasons alone with no higher purpose will not allow true transition to take place. For change to be seen in our life, we must be properly positioned in the seat of transition.

Transition begins when we accept our failure, when we realize we can do nothing without God, and when we embrace what is and let go what was. During my transition stage in life, I had to realize the place I currently existed was a part of where I was headed. Often, we find ourselves in some tough positions, from finances to careers to relationships; life tends to throw a hay-maker that seems to knock us down. The key to transition is embracing what is felt, learning from that feeling, and trusting the Spirit of God to lead us out of the wilderness we have placed ourselves in.

Along that journey out, we will feel a lot of uncomfortable things. Those feelings are there because we are being torn from things that have stagnated our growth. The feeling is not because something is wrong, it is God aligning us with what is promised for us through Christ Jesus.

Transition is not about stripping you from being able to feel, but about stripping you from reacting to life based *solely* on how you feel. This can be so uncomfortable because in a lot of our lives, feelings have controlled our life over God.

When transition has taken root in our lives, thoughts become more mature, responsibility becomes an action instead of a reaction, and emotions become more than just a feeling that we impulsively act on. These are the bare essentials of transition. Please note: transition never fails people, but rather people fail at submitting to transition's proposal for change.

Transition requires us to abandon what we think we know to be receptive to what God has placed before us. This in itself is an obstacle; simply abandoning things we've been accustomed to doing for years is like telling a fish to survive on land. Jeremiah 29:11 says, "For I know the plans I have for you," declares the Lord, "plans to prosper you and not to harm you, plans to give you hope and a future." When our faith rises to this truth of what God says, then our ways are easily let go for something greater.

Transition has phases. Transition deals with impatience, anger, fear, stubbornness, selfishness. These things will always kick against transition as it takes you from one place to another.

Many who have only seen themselves in these things will say, "Well, that is just how I am." Many have believed that. What robs us of peace is our fight against change, and the inability to embrace transition. Transition takes work, and many are not willing to put in the work. So we consciously and unconsciously begin to project a negative attitude toward all we do in life, robbing ourselves of the peace God has already promised.

So the question we must ask ourselves is: What place have you given transition in your life? This process cannot be manipulated unless you manipulate yourself. True spiritual effort is the best one, while a mind that refutes understanding is paralyzed. Embracing transition and the phases one may go through is the key to change in our spiritual walk in life. We cannot change transition, but we must learn the phases of transition and let what is revealed change us. We must not look back at what was and miss all the joy that lies ahead. Prepare to take your position, so God can better you through your transition and teach you who you are in Christ.

ASK YOURSELF...

1. What are some examples of life transitions you have undertaken in the past?

2. Is transition a natural state for you, or do you fight change every step of the way? Why do you think that is?

3. When change is necessary, who can you call on to support you along the journey?

4. What area of your life is in transition now, or should be?

CHAPTER 3 :: DAY 13
It's Not the Moment, but the Opportunity the Moment Presents

We are often encouraged to 'live in the moment.' Moments in our lives happen for a reason, but the question I challenge you with is this: Is living in the moment more important than seizing the opportunity the moment presents?

Luke 4:5 says, "The devil led him up to a high place and showed him in an instant all the kingdoms of the world."

In this moment of life, Jesus could have seen this and decided to say "okay." Instead, Jesus knew the future was more important than that moment. When we decide that specific moments in life are more important than future goals, our emotions have taken control of how we spiritually need to view things. At no point am I saying you should not feel or enjoy certain times in your life, I am simply saying the moments in life are only the start, and if the feeling of that moment clouds our spiritual eye, we may miss the opportunity the moment presents.

When Satan tempted Jesus in that moment, the Lord said, 'Thanks but no thanks.' The opportunity for saving the world was greater than what would have only satisfied momentary feelings.

College students, while partying, say, 'I am living my best life.' A mother giving birth enjoys the moment of her child being born. Two completely different scenarios, but each one also similar. A moment for their emotions, but also an opportunity for life. By resting in the feeling of that moment, we will only see what our emotions want us to see. Sometimes we struggle with trusting the Spirit over what our natural mind says, and what others want us to feel. The college student, if not careful, will enjoy the moment so much that focus is lost and the opportunity of a better life is put in jeopardy with each moment that is placed in front of purpose. A new mother, in the moment of having a child, basks in attention for too long, losing sight of the important things in life that child needs to know.

What am I saying? The feelings we have in the big moments of our life, if not placed in their proper position, will cause us to not capitalize on the opportunity of purpose that came wrapped in those moments. The enemy wants us to keep our eyes on the world so we can be drawn away. The enemy does not mind your child going off to college, but he does not want them to change the world. The enemy does not mind you giving birth to a child, but he does not want that child to be raised fearing Jesus. So the enemy will use our feelings in moments so the opportunity of truly abundant life is lost.

Many will fall short a time or two, but how long will you live in the moment, rather than enrich the opportunity the moment is presenting? There comes a point in life when we all have to be still, and come to that point of truth. That moment, whatever that may look like to you, is your opportunity to let truth reign.

Have you gotten 'stuck' in certain moments of life longer than is healthy for you? How long has the loss of a loved one kept you bound? How long has bitterness in a relationship stunted your marriage? How long has anger kept families torn apart? It all starts with a moment.

We must stop becoming moment chasers — so lost to opportunity that we run and hide in each moment that seems to feed feelings that are created out of a lie. We should enjoy life, but we must enjoy life responsibly, with respect for self and others.

I don't want anyone to stop living; I want us all to live with purpose. There are many moments, but not a lot of time.

A wide window of awakening, but not many willing to be receptive to that awakening. So embrace moments, but don't live in them. Step back, trust God, and acknowledge Him in all you do so you can see the opportunity for elevation in your life that each moment presents.

ASK YOURSELF...

1. Do you live for the next big moment? If so, what does this look like in your life?

2. Is it possible you are missing out on a deeper relationship with God, or pursuing your true purpose, because you are too focused on temporary moments of happiness?

3. What can you do to slow down, engage with life on a deeper level, and place your eyes more firmly on Jesus, beyond the temporary?

4. Where do you feel stuck, in life? Have you given these stuck places over to God in prayer?

CHAPTER 3 :: DAY 14
Proper Perspective

Proper perspective in life must be established in a conscious state of mind, or anything else in our vision will be blocked. What do I mean by 'conscious?' In order to see life in its proper perspective, we must be properly aligned, consciously aware of how the Word of God plays a significant role in our outlook on life.

How can a mind that is delusional, or a heart that is weighed down with pain and bitterness, ever hope to have proper perspective? And how can a mind that is consumed with family issues, kids, bills, jobs, and other forms of responsibility, develop peace, in order to see what God has in store for their lives?

The constant turning of life, and the things that are part of our lives, can make peace almost impossible to attain, but all things are possible with God. We need not search for peace, for it lies within us: greater is He who lives within you, than he who is in the world. Poor decisions may place us in harsh circumstances, and in these dark places our perspective can become destructive.

In many cases, the problems we face in life begin with us. Simply because we allowed the mistake, the pain, the frustration — to become us. The moment this happens, we begin to lose self. Proper perspective is established in truth, while destructive perspective is rooted in self-supported lies. Lies we tell ourselves that make us project all the negativity that rests in our hearts onto others, which changes our whole perspective on life. Every negative or painful thing that happens in our lives can be conquered by the voice of peace, if we allow it.

That doesn't mean peace will simply make you forget the hurt, but it will give you the proper perspective to deal effectively with the pain. Quick solutions and trying to fill a void instantaneously only makes us *think* the pain is gone — an illusion that only serves to stagnate our spiritual growth.

Frustration will come, pain will exist, stress will threaten to overcome us, but peace is waiting to release us. Peace that allows us to see the situation clearly, and to react based on spiritual knowledge, and not simply on our feelings.

To maintain a proper perspective on life, we must have a strong sense of self control, which is one of the fruits of the spirit. When we allow the temporary circumstances of our lives to control us, we lose our identity in Christ. True purpose is found when we cultivate a mature spiritual perspective on life.

We should focus on building up proper spiritual perspective — not just for our own success, but for the growth and fulfillment of others.

ASK YOURSELF...

1. What are your biggest frustrations or challenges in life right now?

2. Be honest with yourself: When you consider these challenges are you viewing them through 'worldly eyes' or through a spiritual lens?

3. As believers, our eyes are trained toward eternity; given the temporary nature of the problems in life, which ones can you hand over to God in prayer, asking Him to help you tackle these problems?

4. As you begin to develop a more mature spiritual perspective, who else can you support? Who can you share your perspective with in order to inspire someone else to seek new perspective in the Lord?

CHAPTER 3 :: DAY 15
Sound the Alarm

The book of Joel is a powerful book in the Bible. Joel lets the people of Judah know what is coming to them for their disobedience if they do not repent.

Joel 2:1 says, "Blow the trumpet in Zion; sound the alarm on my holy hill. Let all who live in the land tremble, for the day of the Lord is coming. It is close at hand."

You may tie an alarm to an alarm clock to wake you up, or you may connect an alarm to a sound that means "warning: something is about to happen or has already happened." Either way, when an alarm is set it is saying get ready. Too often, we hear the alarm in our lives but just like when an alarm goes off when we are asleep — we roll over and turn the alarm off.

Stop and think...how many alarms have we turned off in our lives? What do I mean? The alarm of division that seems to creep up due to pride and a lack of forgiveness. The alarm of spiritual relationship, that things of this world have grown far too important to us. The alarm of injustice on all levels. These types of alarms go off daily, but we tend to roll over and stay asleep to the solution, only waking up when it is too late.

We must wake up to the grace and mercy we have been given through Christ Jesus so we can begin to set the alarm for peace, for love, and for unity — instead of reacting to alarms that go off because we have been disobedient to the call.

When an alarm goes off, it serves as a reminder of what is needed to respond to. Our minds are alarms that if transformed by the Word of God, can react to worldly situations according to biblical truth instead of worldly perception. Whatever our minds are set to when natural things happen in life, an alarm goes off and our focus determines how we are impacted, and what choices we make.

Too many harbored bad memories may cause a negative reaction.

When a family member passes, when bills pile up, when life seems unfair, one alarm triggers another and if our minds are set on the world more than God, we may miss the call to something greater. There comes a point in life when we must sound the alarm, because we have been in pain too long. We have been thrown guilt too long. We have been thrown doubt too long. We have lived in sin too long. Life can be cruel and seem to be more of a curse than a blessing at times. But much like Joel sounded the alarm to warn those around him to change their course, there is a better way than the route you are going.

God is gracious enough today to set those alarms off, but our minds must be in tune with those alarms, and allow opportunities to come from what is being set rather than turn into what a situation or circumstance says we should be. We must stop putting God on silent, and then wonder why we seem to walk around in life with no sense of direction.

Whether believers or non-believers, we must stop turning over to the alarms that God is setting in our lives to bring us to a higher calling and deeper experience of peace. Only you know what alarms in your life you have been ignoring. It is time to ring the alarm that says I have been doing this too long. Submit to the mighty hand of God so your life can be filled with the peace you have always desired.

Are you ready to wake up or will you continue to silent the alarm and stay asleep?

ASK YOURSELF...

1. What circumstances in life ring 'alarm bells' for you?

2. When faced with a stressful situation or challenge, do you bury your head in the sand, attempt to go it alone, or turn to God?

3. In what areas of your life do you think God is trying to get your attention?

4. Tune your hearing to the One who has a plan for your life. What is the first area of your life you can hand over to God, trusting His plan and listening for His guidance in this area?

An Introduction to Chapter 4

The letter I received from my mom gave me renewed life, and I felt really good. I was unaware at the time that this was only the beginning of building proper friendships and relationships in my life. I prayed a prayer one night before I was getting ready to leave solitary confinement and return to general population — which meant I would be housed with other people.

This move was exciting and scary at the same time. For two years, I had not had to deal with anyone but myself. The prayer that I prayed was "Please Lord God take the people out of my life that mean me no good, and place people in my life who do." I had no idea that God had already removed all the things that would hinder me from developing positive, healthy friendships and relationships.

In the prison environment, it is not always easy to establish good friendships, or to develop healthy relationships with family and loved ones. Although I was seeing things in different ways, each new step in life was a reminder of what was already established. Our memories aren't erased, but the more positive things we place in front of the negative, the harder it is to return to a negative viewpoint.

God is a God of restoration. I still had a hard time trying to figure out how God wanted me to build friendships while in prison. My eyes were opened when I met a guy by the name of Jihad, a man who had a life sentence and was of a different faith than me.

Jihad asked me one day, "How do you stay positive in this environment?" I told him I cultivated a positive attitude by separating my physical incarceration from my mental, emotional, and spiritual freedom. From that point, two people from different walks of life and different beliefs were able to form a friendship that still exists today.

Through helping people, I learned valuable skills that allowed me on this leg of the journey to see friendship and relationships in a different way.

We are almost there — don't give up. Now lets go!

CHAPTER

FOUR

FRIENDSHIPS and RELATIONSHIPS

CHAPTER 4 :: DAY 16
Egos: Relationships and True Relationships

These two words: "relationship" and "friendship," are two of the most misrepresented words in the world we live in today. We have devalued the true meaning of each one. Social media has redefined both, and has made many gravitate to the new meaning. The new definition of 'friend' is anyone who likes a post, and a relationship is considered one who likes all that is only seen on the surface of a person. Relationships and friendships have been rooted in ego.

Ego can be defined as "a person's sense of self-importance." As we look around today, many relationships and friendships, whether personal or business, have been built on self-importance. When we are in a relationship with a significant other, or just developing a friendship, we must ask ourselves, "Is this friendship or relationship true or formulated from my ego?"

We must have a clear understanding of the ego in order to know how to build fruitful friendships and relationships. The ego is everything you want it to be. It is built for you when reality is not panning out how you would like it to. We build egos to protect ourselves from feeling pain, and we project onto others what the ego needs.

True relationships identify themselves with only what is present, while ego-built relationships want the past to be remembered — to make everything in your present pay for what happened in the past. Of course, not one time in the Bible do we see the word "relationships," but all throughout the Bible we see examples of true relationships. Jesus had a relationship with His Father, God, which allowed him to have a fruitful relationship with his disciples.

John 13:5 says, "After that, he poured water into a basin and began to wash his disciples' feet, drying them with the towel that was wrapped around him."

This is true relationship. The word relationship is not just tied to a title, but to actions that uphold the title. Jesus is King of Kings and

Lord of Lords, yet He humbled Himself to show His appreciation of His disciples. This is an action of true relationship. A willingness to put self to the side to uplift those you love.

The ego upholds title with no regard to the ones you love, because the love of self supersedes all things. We sometimes build relationships in an attempt to hide pain, building up the ego in hopes that the relationship will heal our pain — all at the emotional, mental, and spiritual expense of another. So a fabricated love is formed, and in time, we begin to believe we truly love another person when the only thing that is really loved is the fact that the relationship is serving as a power source to charge our ego.

So how does ego enter a relationship? It enters through the heart being open to all that ego offers: selfishness, pride, and worldly pleasures; when a heart is inclined to these things, regardless of how a relationship starts, the ego will eventually take full control. This is why fifty-percent of marriages end in divorce, because self-importance becomes more important than the actions that support the union.

Jesus knew that it was never about Him — it was all about fulfilling the work of His Father. We too can learn from this: It is not all about us in a relationship; it is about how we, too, can be like Jesus and humble ourselves to serve another, regardless of how much power we may have.

You may say, "Well, I don't want anyone walking all over me." Nobody wants that! Jesus was betrayed already in the heart of Judas, but He still honored this relationship. If Jesus had allowed Judas' feeling to capture His attention because of ego, it would have pulled Him away from the greater purpose of God's plan. We cannot allow our feelings to pull us deeper into the hold of our ego.

True relationships are built for the bettering of another, not just ourselves. It is our ability to overcome pain, help others, and see beauty in another that true relationships are built upon, strongly rooted, and established.

True relationships can only exist if you allow them to. True relationships will endure trial and hardship, because the attention is not on the problem, but the solution. This is not a fairytale world; people are cruel, but if you allow the cruelty of others to change you, in time you will become just as cruel as them, missing the beauty found in true relationship.

Once a true relationship is deeply rooted, the things needed to sustain it will flow, and ego will have no place — so it must go.

Will you allow true relationship to take root in your life, or has ego built a prison within you that blocks you from seeing the peace, love, and joy that come from true relationships? Healing and restoration begin with being honest with yourself about your past relationships, your current relationships, and the kind of relationships you want to build in the future.

Are you ready for that?

ASK YOURSELF...

1. How many true relationships do you have, that go deeper than surface 'friendships' on social media?

2. Consider one or two of your most important relationships with others; are these relationships balanced, with both sides contributing equally? If not, are you giving more or taking more from these relationships?

3. The ability to build someone up in a relationship requires setting aside your own ego in order to prioritize the needs of another. Have you struggled with ego in the past? How does ego impact your relationships now?

4. Jesus, King of Kings and Lord of Lords, humbled Himself to wash the feet of His disciples. How can you display this kind of humility and willingness to serve in your own relationships? Be specific.

CHAPTER 4 :: DAY 17
The Confusion of a Union

James 1:8 says, "A double-minded man is unstable in all his ways." Many of us read this verse with no idea how it applies to our life, but quickly point it out in another's life. When two individuals on any level come together, both parties must be willing to reciprocate each others' efforts in their own gifted way. A lack of this, and the union becomes unbalanced. How many of us have formed unions based on how it can advance us superficially? Or better yet, how many of us have formed unions that cater to our own motives? Jesus has a deep relationship with His Father. Based on that connection, He was able to connect meaningfully with others — even those who opposed Him.

Every person in any friendship or relationship has a wide range of potential. Too often, people tend not to pay attention to the negative things that can cause a rift, until it affects their emotional standing. When this occurs it is too late to save the relationship; too many things have transpired that cause spiritual awareness to be replaced with selfish ambition rooted in disturbed emotion. At that point, we focus more on the damage done than on the root cause, leaving little room to find a solution.

A friend must be there for a friend. Proverbs 17:17 says, "A friend loves at all times, and a brother is born for a time of adversity." The Bible does not say "sometimes," but all times. In a relationship, it is a duty to be there for your mate — even in tough times. By doing this, you do what honors a friendship or a relationship, taking no thought of self, but placing the greater good of the other person above your own wants or needs.

This does not mean you neglect self, but you place another's needs over your own. Confusion comes in when pain from the past is carried and applied to new situations, and unrealistic expectations are placed on the union based on a broken heart and an unstable mind. Past pain in any union can cause one to prey on the vulnerability of the other, clothing themselves in a "sheep's clothing" vulnerability to hide their own insecurity.

You may say, "I will never deal with anyone like that," but we have dealt with and have even been that person at some point unintentionally, but when we were hurt or had pain in our lives. Pain not dealt with is the road to broken emotions, which can give way to confusion in a union. We tend to serve pain as if it is Jesus, forgetting that it is by His lashes we are healed.

In friendships and relationships, we are to help complement our partners strengths, and help them grow when they're weak. Confusion sets in when we make the friendship or relationship all about ourselves. Spiritual balance must be applied, which creates a space where two individuals can uplift one another so that our relationships become fruitful.

Our attraction must be to the Christ in a person. Not sex, money, power, fame, or selfish love to cover up truth...these approaches will always leave us confused and unfulfilled. This truth can make a person become very defensive, not because what is being displayed is wrong, but an observation has been made that one does not want to face. The cycle of confusion starts with pain, then generates doubt, restrains spiritual guidance, and empowers feelings which compromise the friendship or relationship as a whole. This troubled song is placed on repeat for the world to listen to over and over again. So many of us have been hurt, then move on without a solution, and this is why we have so much confusion in our unions.

Seek godliness in others, and work to cultivate Christ in yourself, and you will find greater love, peace, and fulfillment in your relationships with others.

ASK YOURSELF...

1. How have you played a role in the cycle of confusion/frustration in your relationships?

2. Are you ready to face what is causing you to see friendships and relationships in a negative light?

3. Are you ready to trust God with your relationships? Why or why not?

CHAPTER 4 :: DAY 18
Reputation Can't be Built on What You're Going to Do

Can you imagine if Jesus said, "I was going to save you...but I just didn't feel like it?" Or better yet, if God in the garden told Adam, "I was going to save others through My Son, Jesus, but you messed up!" If that were so, it would make the Word of God hard to believe. Thank God for His mercy and grace.

Too often, this is what we do in our friendships and relationships. Then, we wonder why things seem to always end in a negative way. We say or have heard things like, "I am going to be there," "I am going to love you better," "I am going to do better." But there isn't always genuine intent behind these statements. Many of us neglect true friendships and relationships for reputation based on words spoken in good faith.

Is it not true that words are only respected when action, which solidifies reputation, is seen? So, why have many of us in relationships and friendships based what we have on what we are going to do? Then we expect the other individual to bank on words that have no action behind them.

This is acceptable today because spiritual fulfillment has been replaced by temporary fulfillment. As we read through the Bible, every great and worthy leader gained a reputation based on Christ-like character, followed by actions that changed the lives of others. Our acceptance of others today is based on a momentary feeling, not on spiritual happiness and peace as a whole. What we as people choose to accept is based on the standards one has for themselves. There is a saying: Reputation is what people perceive you as, character is who you know you are. As an example, Saul in the Book of Acts has a reputation of killing all the Christians; this is what people of his time perceived him as: a killer of Christians. After his conversion on the road to Damascus (Acts 9:4-6), he began to walk in who he knew he was in Christ. He began to do the opposite of what people thought he would do.

In our relationships, it is not about the reputation you have or had. It is about walking in who you know you are in Christ. A lack of noble character puts one in a position to see reputation before character. Our relationships should not be based on what we think, they should be based on how they will honor God. Our own fickle approach will constantly leave relationships lacking, or even broken. From Abraham to Moses, their reputations were established through proper spiritual character that led to life-changing actions, which in turn changed the lives of others.

It is our duty to help better our friends or our partner based on noble spiritual character, not words that just sound good. Social media has been used as a platform to display a reputation built on half-truths, and people are actually using their social media status to base their worth. Sadly, many people accept individuals' reputations based on what they seem like rather than on reality.

Life-long friendships are being broken, and relationships are being destroyed, because many of us have traded in the character of Christ for a worldly reputation. Some people of poor reputation attempt to mask the truth with meaningless words, but lack the character to make their words a reality. Many think a reputation can be built by hand, hoping it can solidify what they still don't know about themselves. When you know who you are, your character is solidified by your actions — and then reputation is established by what has been done.

Christ-like character produces solid actions, and those actions bring about a good rapport that is dependable.

ASK YOURSELF...

1. Are you content with a reputation built on the things you say, rather than the things you do?

2. What is your definition of a Christ-like character? Seek out specific Bible verses to support this definition.

3. Your reputation — the results of your actions, has a long term impact on others. What kind of legacy do you think your actions (and reputation) are leaving on your current relationships?

4. Describe the reputation you would like to have with your loved ones, friends, and community. What steps can you take to earn this reputation?

CHAPTER 4 :: DAY 19
Friendship

The concept of being a true friend over time has been transformed and viewed more from the receiving end, rather than the giving end.

Many people have gravitated to this because of previous toxic friendships in which they were hurt, and vowed never to be hurt in that manner again. To prevent this pain, many of us have put people through an obstacle course just to be our friend.

Can you imagine if God made us go through a mental, emotional, or spiritual test to be his friend? Although we fail when we are tested at times, God never says, "Okay...I'm done with you." Many of us have created a friendship guideline that in truth only attracts people that keep us insecure, and keep us in pain, thus basing friendship off of what a person can give to help shield us from our own pain.

Many times we reject the people who will serve as good friends, simply because that person causes us to see who we truly are, and many of us do not like that. You might ask, "Who would reject a person who will be honest with you to help make a better you?" Sad to say, that person has been me, and that person has also been you. We have all, at times, judged a new opportunity of true friendship based on a bad previous one.

Proverbs 17:17 says, "A friend loves at all times, and a brother is born for a time of adversity."

Jesus loves us always. He remains a friend even when we don't deserve the purity that comes with His friendship. Every day we wake up we have a friend in Jesus, yet we base true friendship on natural woes rather than spiritual truths. We have missed the mark; we tend to love our friends when it is convenient for us to love them, then turn around and be upset if we feel our friend is not showing us love in the very area we have neglected to show love to them. We become victims to our own self-built prison, which deprives us of living in the freedom of true friendship.

A true friendship requires one thing: YOU! Not just some of you, but *all* of you. I know this because Jesus gave His life for you and me; that is a love that cannot be denied. It is nearly impossible to establish a friendship if you are lost to who you truly are. How can you trust another person if you cannot trust God? How can you want a friend who is loyal if you cannot be loyal to the people God has placed in your life? Proper morals that are needed to establish healthy friendships start with applying good morals in our own lives.

Friendship does not fail us. We fail friendship.

I know God has developed us all with the skills to develop good friendships. I like to look at friendship in this way:

F. R. I. E. N. D.

Friendship

Forgives,
Respects,
Inspires,
Encourages, &
Never
Destroys.

So, when friendship is viewed in a negative way, we have taken our eye off of Christ, projected our own perceptions onto others, and discredited friendship based on pain that we have yet to release.

True lasting healthy friendships still exist today, because despite our painful state, Jesus is still loving us as His own children, and as friends.

Are you alive enough to allow friendship to survive?

ASK YOURSELF...

1. What is your definition of true friendship?

2. Think about a past friendship that turned ugly, or even toxic. What did you contribute to the situation? What pain did you carry into the future after this experience?

3. Are you comfortable accepting honest feedback from your friends — even when it is painful to hear? What can you do to cultivate a culture of honesty within your relationships?

4. What is your friendship with Jesus like? Are there areas you'd like to grow closer to Him? What aspects of this relationship can you translate into your friendships?

CHAPTER 4 :: DAY 20
Relationship

When we consider the word "relationship," many of us tend to see it from the perspective of what we want, rather than what we can bring to it.

When I see this word, I look at the greatest relationship of all time, that between Jesus Christ and God, His Father. For many who may question this affinity, I have realized the association is not in question, but having faith in what we don't understand is. The relationship Jesus has with His Father is honest, real, loyal, authentic in every way.

God sending His only begotten Son so that we may have life is amazing, but even more amazing is Jesus walking in a sinful world in true correlation with God. As we look at the character of this holy relationship, how can we possibly measure up? We are blessed to have and develop healthy relationships, but many fail due to our inability to stay in a one with our Lord and Savior.

We base connections on natural circumstances, on feelings, on material bliss — and then wonder why what we call a 'relationship' doesn't last. We have replaced love with hate, loyalty with selfishness, humility with pride, and relationship with self-centeredness. After we have replaced things that have substance with things that devalue over time, we then discredit the value of our relationships.

Jesus went through so much for us to have a chance to live life, and even in those hard times, He stayed in affinity with His Father.

John 5:30 says, "By myself I can do nothing; I judge only as I hear, and my judgment is just, for I seek not to please myself but him who sent me."

Our relationships must embody the key elements in this verse. Humility, regardless of what is going on, trusting God not just yourself, and trusting who you have been connected to. Without this, you create a relationship that is going to hurt you, and separate you from the most important relationship of all: your personal relationship with God. All relationships must honor Him who allowed us to conjoin in the first place: Jesus Christ.

If what we do honors more of what we want than what God wants for us within the union that is formed, we have devalued the relationship. We must be true in this area of our life, or the things God put here as a blessing will turn into something we avoid because we have changed the true concept of relationship. Are you willing to build a relationship based on Christ or yourself?

ASK YOURSELF...

1. How do you honor the relationships you are in?

2. Would you characterize your current relationships as being based more on your own needs and desires, or based more on godly character, and God's plan for your life?

3. What can you do differently within your most important relationships to bring honor to God?

4. How can you apply the characteristics of the relationship between God the Father, and His Son Jesus, to your own relationships? What would that look like in action?

An Introduction to Chapter 5

The more I learn about myself and come to the knowledge of who I am in Christ, I still seem to struggle with the word 'respect.'

Each step in life caused me to look back over every area in which I've grown. I not only had to have respect for authority that ruled over me at the time, but I had to have enough respect for myself to respect others. This is extremely difficult when you're in an environment where all around you, there's nothing but disrespect. At times it makes you feel like the only way you can get respect is if you disrespect others. Sometimes in life, this is the position we find ourselves in.

When we look at this word "respect," and as you come along this journey, you will see how respect can take different forms as we allow ourselves to see people in different ways; when we expand our perspective, we can uphold this world with integrity.

CHAPTER FIVE

RESPECT

CHAPTER 5 :: DAY 21
Fair Gain

The phrase "fair gain" has become a phrase that many have gravitated to for their own personal preference. Such as a man or woman pursuing someone already in a relationship based on their own low sense of respect for themselves — they feel like it is fair gain. Or a business partner who cuts his partner out of a deal just to add more wealth to his pockets; he or she feels like this is fair gain.

Of course there is nothing fair about pursuing another man or woman's partner, or cutting a business partner out of a deal. The title of this chapter is "Respect," which is a key characteristic needed in order to live a life that is pleasing to the Lord.

The Bible does not use the word respect, instead it uses the word "reverence," a term meaning "to feel respect for." It is key that we tie scriptural truths to everyday words, so we can understand how the word of God is relevant in our daily life.

Hebrews 12:9 says, "Moreover, we have all had human fathers who disciplined us and we respected them for it. How much more should we submit to the Father of Spirits and live?" The writer in this passage poses a question...there are 3,157 question marks in the Bible. I enjoy questions, because they cause us to think. The writer in Hebrews is asking, "Who do you have more of a reverence for — your father on earth, or the God who created it all?" This is the same question we must ask ourselves on this journey. Will we have more respect for our personal approaches to life? Or will our respect be based on how what we do affects our relationship with Christ?

We all know that not all things in life are fair. Fair is a word that can only be defined truly based on one's spiritual state. If we are out of touch with who we are in Christ, we will see fair as a word that applies more to what we want and how we feel, rather than simply having a reverence for God.

If we lack proper spiritual conduct, we will view the most unfair things in life as fair gain, not because they are fair, but because we have made what is wrong, right, to make up for what we feel we lack. With this approach we have lost respect for self and have lost a reverence for God.

You may say, "I have respect for myself." How many times have you applied unfair conduct and called it fair gain, based solely on how it made you feel personally? (Remember — it is only you in the room.) We all have at times acted in ways that resemble a lack of respect for self. That fact is not the problem, the problem is that many of us choose to stay in that state, and fail to see how that stagnates us in life.

True gain is responding to situations in life with a firm reverence for God, respect for self, and a respect for others despite their actions, because it is not their actions you have respect for, but the Christ that is in them despite how ugly they seem to be.

In closing some may say, "Well it all sounds good but on this journey of mine you can't always get ahead by acting right." You may feel that is true, but who is to say that those you do see get ahead by not having a reverence for God have peace? Despite their superficial standpoint, can you say without a doubt that they are happy? Where there is no reverence for God there is no reverence for life. When we personalize life and base everything off of our own outlook, and make what is unfair, fair gain, we have not only lost respect for ourselves — we have lost our reverence for our Lord and Savior Jesus Christ, and that is a state that we should all be in fear of being in.

ASK YOURSELF...

1. Have you ever profited unfairly, whether that profit is emotional, or in the form of tangible or material wealth? How did you feel about those gains?

2. Describe a "fair" situation you've been involved in. Now, describe an "unfair" situation you've been part of. What did you learn from each of these circumstances?

3. Do you respect yourself enough to treat others with fairness? Why or why not?

4. What is more important, getting ahead, or acting with integrity? Why do you feel this way?

CHAPTER 5 :: DAY 22
Respecting the Not So Obvious

People tend to value respect on circumstantial evidence alone, wanting desperately to respect something or someone for any reason. Not for any particular reason other than to say that we have a clear understanding of the word discipline. We live in a time where many of us respect only the obvious that in many cases only appeals to the monetary things in life.

Many respect LeBron James for his ability, as well as his off the court bravery. Obama for his leadership. And any other influential figure based on the obvious things that are seen. All they do should be respected indeed, and in these cases it is easy to respect a person or a situation, when everything about them looks good.

So the question is, are you willing to invest in respect even when it is not so obvious? Yes, respect is an action word; however, it is not the action alone that should be respected, but the process one goes through that allows those actions to be seen.

Many of us respect emotions more than the evaluation of their emotions, many respect nice things, and not what it took to get those nice things. Many of us believers have a reverence for Christ, but we neglect all the not so obvious things Jesus suffered. We read about what He went through, but do we have a reverence for the patience Jesus displayed when the disciples continued to ask questions, continued to have disbelief, fear, doubt… Without Jesus' journey we would not begin to respect the obvious death and resurrection that many of us do today.

Respect does not start from the top down, but from the bottom up. We must respect in ourselves, as well as others, the pain that was overcome, and all the let-downs along the way. Can you imagine how Jesus felt when He told Peter that he would deny Him three times (Matthew 26:34-35)? Yet He still died for Peter, and for all of us. At times we just think that is what Jesus was supposed to do, but our respect should be in Christ's ability to not trust how betrayal would make Him feel, but He rested in overcoming betrayal with love.

When we only respect the obvious we neglect the process, when in fact the obvious may not be as respected if we saw the road it traveled. If we dilute respect and base it solely on what we see, we strive to obtain respect based on possession and not purpose. We must live a life rooted in reverence for the Lord, that displays a light that shines not on what people do for respect, but the substance in the journey.

It is what people don't see — the unapparent things — the pain, the dark nights, the tears that hit the pillow nobody saw, the points when giving up seemed more profitable than keeping on. The less obvious things are the hardships that you've endured alone. Our duty is to live a life full of respect just like Jesus. We are not defined by the things that people choose to respect us for, but for the hardship that groomed us in respect that leads to a life full of substance, in honor to God. This, in turn, leads to a life that exudes respect so one will never have to seek it to know their worth.

ASK YOURSELF...

1. How have you respected the less obvious things in your life?

2. Give an example of someone you respect or admire. Why do you look up to this person?

3. Dig deeper. This person was not born a great athlete, or leader, or manager, or parent, or pastor. Learn more about their story. Did they struggle along the way? What obstacles did they overcome?

4. What does learning more about someone else's struggle, teach you about yourself?

CHAPTER 5 :: DAY 23
It Is Not Who You Know, But Who Knows You

When dealing with this topic I want to briefly pay attention to the word "know." A synonym for this word is to perceive, discern, to "understand." As life goes on, the people you know may have a sound understanding of who they are, but the question is does that person or group know you?

When we look at a lot of successful stories, their success is not rooted in who they know, but rather who knows them. Scripture states in 1 Corinthians 8:3, "But if any man love God, the same is known of him." When our Lord and Savior knows you by name, that is a relationship that trumps any natural relationship one may have.

Many people may have taken the time to understand you as a person, at times for manipulative reasons — for example to use knowing you as a bargaining chip, or a friendship that is just good for a certain amount of time. But when your love for Jesus is established it is not about who you know, but who knows you, because others will see the Christ in you. They will not only have respect for you, but more importantly, they will have respect for the Christ in you.

When a person knows you, they have knowledge of who you are not just superficially, but who you are within. When Jesus is the love of our life He knows all we need. When Jesus knows you, it is not about who you know.

Too often we try to know the right people, thinking by knowing the right people it puts us in good graces with others. Personally, in trying to know the right people, I only found myself connected to the wrong people.

When we think we know what we need better than God already knows, we stagnate our growth. Although the superficial things can be gratifying based on who you know, those relationships will never be able to give you more than Jesus.

Why is it important for someone to know you? A person who knows you with understanding, appreciates and has knowledge of who you are — flaws and all. Our identity is in Christ, and God brings us relationships with all who need to be in our lives, because we are loved that much by our Lord and Savior, and the respect he has for us is beyond our own comprehension.

Our power lies in knowing that Jesus knows us by name. How we carry ourselves, how we treat people, our stories, our courage, our strength, our love for Christ will speak in tones that will be understood and "respected."

So I encourage you not to put yourself in good graces just to say you know someone of significance. We must be sure that people know us based on our love for Christ, and in knowing Christ, God knows what we need (Matthew 6:8).

When our love for Christ is the center of our life, God respects us and through Christ, respect will be given to us and all we do.

ASK YOURSELF...

1. Have you allowed Christ to truly know you?

2. Do you fit in with the "right" crowd? Does this really matter? Why or why not?

3. Who knows you best? Does this person respect you? Why or why not?

4. What are you known for? Does your relationship with Jesus, play into the reputation you have in your family or among your peers?

CHAPTER 5 :: DAY 24
Respect Is Yours

Respect has no limit, and the value we put on respect is based on our reverence for Christ. Respect is yours, because when Jesus died on the cross and rose from the grave, the respect He walked in was imparted unto you.

Nobody can rob you of respect when you know who you are, and who you are in Christ. No man can take what has been imparted unto you.

For many years I had lost respect for life, because I lost who I was in Christ. So, I personalized respect, I placed standards on respect, I placed expectations on respect, as if the word respect held the power alone to make me feel better. I placed rules on respect that stood upon my own thinking, and had nothing to do with God.

As believers in Christ, we come to points in our life that we want respect to serve us, rather than serving respect. As believers in Christ we have been given the foundation of respect, everything that defines respect lies in Christ, but we must not abuse what by grace we have obtained. Yes, respect is yours — there is no circumstance, no pain, no fear, that can take that from you. Respect is yours through Christ Jesus.

We are publishers of respect, but we must never forget we are not the author of it. We are not the creators of the word respect; we are but vessels that can carry out the true meaning of the word.

Although respect is ours through Christ Jesus, it is our choice what we do with this respect. Will we honor what Christ has given, or will we redefine it based on how we feel we have or have not been respected?

At no point am I saying to just let people treat you any kind of way; in 2 Timothy 1:7 the Word of God states, "For God hath not given us the spirit of fear; but of power, and of love, and of a sound mind."

When disrespect is in our presence, it has no power over us. Our Lord and Savior, despite our sin, holds us in the light of respect. Christ has a deep admiration for those who believe in Him, because he looks not on what people see, but at the abilities and qualities within us.

Knowing that respect is yours should give you a sense of ownership. Life has its advantages and disadvantages. Being an owner of something, we are responsible for the negative and the positive that comes from how we represent what we are co-owners of.

When we devalue respect, we will project that same value to others as well as ourselves. The devaluing of respect comes from basing our ownership of respect off what we feel and think, rather than who we know we are in Christ.

We can never lean upon our own understanding, we must in all our ways acknowledge Him (Proverbs 3:5-6). Respect has a certain amount of nobility that each individual should hold within themselves. The lack of this makes one a poor owner of something with so much potential. Bonds are broken, and people are hurt because people are owners of the word respect, and only want to apply it when it benefits them.

Respect is yours, but how have you allowed it to be seen and passed on? Respect is yours as long as you uphold the foundation respect is built on, which is Jesus Christ. We can be the owner of something and not understand the power of its use. Yes, respect is yours, but the question is are you allowing this ownership to help you or hurt you?

ASK YOURSELF...

1. How have you respected what is yours? How have you respected life? How have you respected yourself?

2. Who do you offer respect to? Do you do this because this person is worthy, or because there is something to gain from the situation?

3. Respect is a noble habit to cultivate. In what areas of your life do you need to strengthen your respect muscle?

4. What would you like to be respected for? Do you seek respect for qualities of character, or the temporary trappings of the world such as money, fame, or status?

CHAPTER 5 :: DAY 25
Living Respect

Respect is a word that a lot of people demand out of others, but lack that same demand from self. The so-called motto that many have gravitated to is "To get respect you must give respect." The motto serves no purpose to those who believe this, if an individual sees respect, but fails to live respect from the foundation respect stands on. The motto was only created to make one feel safe in restricting others from receiving respect based on a feeling. So the motto might as well be "If I feel like respecting you, I will."

Living respect is discussed in Philippians 4:8, "Finally, brethren, whatsoever things are honest, whatsoever things are just, whatsoever things are pure, whatsoever things are lovely, whatsoever things are of good report; if there be any virtue, and if there be any praise, think on these things."

Respect stands on these characteristics. Too often we allow how we feel about matters to determine whether we will live a life of respect. How we feel takes more precedence than our reverence for God, our respect for others, and finally respect for ourselves. The lack of self-control--part of the fruit of the Spirit--and emotional instability makes respect an act of *choice*, rather than something you want to give despite someone's behavior. Our reverence for God is what we honor.

Every individual in life deserves respect; I say that because an unstable mind can never know respect unless they see it, a child cannot learn certain things if they are not taught. If we neglect to display respect on all levels it stagnates another as well as ourselves. Some may say how is the lack of another placed on me? It is not that we are responsible for their life, but we are responsible for standing on Philippians 4:8, and being a vessel that respect can be seen from. This is not a message meant to condemn or to confuse, but a message to open our spiritual eyes to the importance of respect that starts with a reverence for God first, so we can better respect others and ourselves in a way that pleases God and not the world or our own selfish motives.

There are many things in our own lives we know would not honor God. So if we know that, how can we disrespect another for a flaw that we ourselves have hidden? Living respect allows one to see past the things that are not, so we can see all the things that are through the eyes of Christ — in others as well as ourselves.

Are you willing to live respect that gives reverence to God, and show respect for others, which allows us to respect life and live life in the peace of God?

ASK YOURSELF...

1. How does the world define respect?

2. How do you personally define respect?

3. Are you actively living out an attitude of respect? How might you encourage growth in this area?

4. Is respect for self, and others, an area where you find peace? How might inviting God to be part of this issue help?

An Introduction to Chapter 6

For many years, I thought time had stopped — at least for me. In my situation, in a certain way, it did. The opportunity to spend time with my children, the opportunity to spend time with my family, was lost due to my inability to embrace and understand all that has been discussed in the previous chapters.

Feeling like I lost my spirit when I was molested, feeling abandoned by my family, feeling like life had turned on me, every friend and relationship that was developed was developed out of pain, and I never had respect for myself, which brings me to time.

Although at this point, time may have been paused from interacting with society because for the first time, I was not just existing, but I was actually living. I was able to understand the importance of life, and that is what we have to do when we've lost so much.

We must embrace time, not just exist in it, but live so that each day that we spend with family and loved ones can be spent wisely.

Sometimes we wait too late to appreciate and value the time that we have.

CHAPTER SIX

TIME

CHAPTER 6 :: DAY 26
Silent Breath

There are silent breaths taken within time that we must be aware of.

A car accident happens. A close family member dies.
A deep breath is taken.
Or in my case, where I was molested at an early age.
A deep breath was taken.
Being hurt by a person that you thought you would spend the rest of your life with.
A deep breath is taken.

At these times in our lives, a deep breath is taken and we don't even realize the breath has been taken. Sad but true — when we take those deep breaths, it takes time for us to breathe yet again. Some may say, "You cannot hold your breath that long or you will die!" From a natural standpoint that may be correct, but from a spiritual position that deep breath can begin to suffocate our spiritual life.

Ecclesiastes 3:1 says, "To every thing there is a season, and a TIME to every purpose under the heavens." Each situation above has the chance to change the way we live, and time is filled with these moments. A family member dies, a child may lose their ability to walk, the pain and the silent breaths that are breathed in those moments have the ability to keep us there, to the point that we do not want to live outside that moment, and we begin to lose time and become stuck in that moment.

We will know when we have taken that deep breath, because anything outside of what caused that breath will make us feel uncomfortable. So unconsciously for months, sometimes years, we base life on that one breath — that one situation that could not be avoided. If that deep breath was taken in pain, it begins to engulf you; if that deep breath was connected to regret, it consumes you; if that deep breath was tied to selfishness, it consumes you.

So when do we breathe again? We exhale that breath when we realize that all things work for the good of those who love the Lord, which allows us to see how much we have allowed a situation to keep us from living a life that gives honor to God.

Just as we can not live without air we cannot live if we do not inhale, the opportunities that are placed in front of us in life become better, despite what situation may have happened. When we see the peace that comes to those who pass away, we can breathe again. When a relationship does not work, we can see the direction God wants us to go, and we can breathe again.

Embrace all that happens in time, but we cannot live in moments of time that will only keep us in a place that robs us of the time we could use to do what God has planned for us.

When life sends blows that seem to knock us out, we cannot get stuck in that time that will only lead to suffocation. We must see what God is doing in that time and breathe.

ASK YOURSELF...

1. What moment or situation in your life — caused you to hold your breath? Is it possible you are still 'holding your breath' in response?

2. Is it possible you have allowed yourself to hold your breath because you can't bear to let go of the pain of the past, or allow yourself to heal after the loss of a relationship or loved one?

3. Imagine the feeling of suffocating slowly. Now picture living with this feeling for months, or even years. What stuck place can you hand over to God, asking Him to help you breathe freely once again?

4. Who do you know who might be stuck? How can you pray for their release from this stuck place?

CHAPTER 6 :: DAY 27
Let Go When Time Expires

Ecclesiastes Chapter 3 speaks very prophetically about time. Time is a very essential thing we have in life, that many tend to take for granted. Time gives us an opportunity to reflect on life. Being consumed with life's everyday demands and responsibilities, reflection is not as admired as it should be.

Everyone comes to knowledge of who they are in Christ at different points in their life. Once one comes to that knowledge, time seems to serve more as an enemy than a friend. Why? Time serves as a friend because it allows us to grow, but can seem to be an enemy when in time we feel or expect our growth to take us to a certain place, or expect because we are at a certain point, then others should be at that point as well.

Time deals with people's growth differently for a reason; each second in life, one door opens and another closes. Instead of understanding this, we continue to try to open doors that in time were meant to be closed. Closed because in time we have outgrown certain things, and God wants to take us to higher places. We stagnate our own growth by holding on to unhealthy relationships, holding on to pain of lost loved ones, holding on to dreams that we have not put enough effort toward achieving because we are afraid to let go of expired things.

How many things are you holding onto that you know time has expired on? It is hard for us to let go of certain things, because we develop a mind that says "well I don't want to fail at this," or we just feel we can fix everything. Time allows us to see, whether we want to or not, the things that are hindering us from growing. When we neglect to see this truth, we begin to rush to catch up to unneeded things, hoping time is on our side, failing to see that time has always been on our side — we have simply neglected to respect and see the opportunities time has given.

The question is no longer what are we holding onto that time has revealed it is time to let go of, but how long will we continue to hold onto expired ideals?

Everyone's journey in life is different, each path is set for them. Dead time is holding on to things that have extended past their expiration date. The more we hold on to these things, the longer we spoil the time we have to be great, make great works, and live in the fullness of God.

Time grants us the opportunity to overcome, move on, and grow. If we refuse to take advantage of what time gives, all we will ever see is what time takes away.

Time is a very precious gift, so appreciate your present. When time speaks — listen, because when time is up there are no second chances.

ASK YOURSELF...

1. What area(s) of life are you holding onto that have reached or passed their expiration dates?

2. When it comes to time, do you set your own schedule, or do you invite God to set things up according to His plans for you, and according to His own timetable?

3. If you had "all the time in the world," how would you spend it?

4. In what areas of your life have you been able to grow, but only with the passing of time?

CHAPTER 6 :: DAY 28
The Essence of Time

Ecclesiastes Chapter 3 speaks of time in a very deep way, which is the foundation of each time passage. Time is significant. Time is what gives each person in life an opportunity to live. Time can be an enemy, time can be a friend, time can be many things — but one thing time cannot be is wasted. Some of us may say "Well people waste time more than you think." But we must ask ourselves in those moments, "Am I hurting time, or am I hurting myself?"

Time is not biased, and time has no set schedule. Time does not judge and time does not fear; time gives us the opportunity to face our fears. The fear of failure, of feeling pain, of losing a loved one; time allows each one of these potential fears to be faced and overcome. Many may say "Well how can you say that?" And the answer to that is very simple: each one of those things mentioned can only be overcome by the essence of time.

Every physical scar takes time to heal properly. If we neglect to give the wound what it needs, we will risk the possibility of that wound being infected. If we infect ourselves with procrastination, wallowing in fear or regret, the spiritual man can never grow. Our lives become scarred when we fail to use our time wisely, when it comes to facing obstacles that are placed in our lives.

Understanding comes when we realize that we will not always make the right choice in life. Seeking God's guidance in our lack of understanding of certain things in our lives is what allows us to value the time we have. Time gives each individual in life a chance to face self as well as the circumstance or situation that can cause one to lose themselves in time.

When we realize how important the essence of time is, nothing can make us second guess if we spent our time wisely. Every second of every day cannot be strategically planned, but every second of every day you can appreciate time.

The time we have to laugh; the time we have to say I love you to a child or loved one; the time we have to accomplish goals; the time we have to say "I am sorry." Despite mistakes and emotional feelings, we have the time to live life without having to live it in fear, for God did not give us a spirit of fear.

ASK YOURSELF...

1. Do you accept and appreciate the miraculous essence of time, or do you waste it?

2. What is the best way you spend your time, currently? What is the most wasteful use of your time?

3. Have you ever offered your time directly to God, asking Him to spend it on whatever He would have you do?

4. Do you truly appreciate the time you've been given? What can you do today to show God your gratitude for the blessing of time?

CHAPTER 6 :: DAY 29
The Elimination of Time

Time is noble. Time can present a state of solitude. Time is not biased. Time was structured to create opportunity. But oh — how times have changed!

Many people cannot stand the reality of time; we have reinvented time to fit our liking. When we try to restructure time, we try to stop and postpone what can never be stopped. Many inventions have been created to hide the look of an aging face, different procedures to hide the slump of an aging body. Everyone pays attention to the external, and tries to change what in time was not meant to change.

Time tends to become a measurement of superficial gain that eventually loses value. Proper functions become problems, because the carnal self is afraid of the truth time will reveal. Every second in life an opportunity is presented, every half second an opportunity is lost. Lost before it can even have a chance, because time for self was more important than time for purpose.

Many times we make time for ourselves not for the betterment, but we make time for ourselves that at times place foolish things in front of impactful things that can change others, as well as ourselves, in time.

So time, then, becomes something that is not cherished, but something that is feared. We begin to race! "How much money can I make?" "How many possessions can I obtain?" And the list goes on and on.

At times we think we own time. In that moment a loved one passes, a relationship ends, a career is lost, a daughter becomes pregnant at an early age. Time reveals it cannot be owned, and it cannot be eliminated.

We must be honest with ourselves. Have we made it past that half a second? The value that one second holds is far beyond anything we can ever imagine. That second that presents opportunity allows us to see self beyond our own insecurities. Time is permitted to allow you to know life has no limit, not to limit yourself, but to discover yourself, not to hinder yourself, but to elevate yourself.

When we realize that time was made by God, we will walk in time with purpose, instead of trying to find ways to eliminate time's purpose. When we respect time we have no regrets, our purpose in life is defined more and more.

Respect of time brings so much peace to ones life. Time is not just another notch on the clock, time is not that which you think is owed to you. Time is a gift given by the grace of God, so we must honor God in time, so we can add peace to our lives and the lives of others.

ASK YOURSELF...

1. How do you feel about the passage of time? Does the ticking of a clock grate on your nerves, or do you accept the passing of time with a sense of peace in your heart? Why?

2. If you could speed up or slow down time, would you? What specific situation(s) would you apply this to?

3. One aspect of character time demands of us is patience. Do you consider yourself a patient person? Why or why not?

4. Are you using the time you have purposefully? Give an example.

CHAPTER 6 :: DAY 30
Losing Track of Time

At times, life consists of so many things that we as people don't pay attention to.

For twenty-two years, I thought life was about money, women, and partying — without a clue to who I was. Yes we must learn from our mistakes, but there are so many still stuck in that stage as full grown adults with the desire to fulfill their emotions, and emotions become bigger than life, and after a repeated cycle we become consumed by our own emotions. Purpose, meaning, spiritual peace, become secondary, and the desire to have fun is the excuse we give ourselves.

In this state the question we must ask ourselves is, "As time passes and twenty-five turns to twenty-eight, and twenty-eight turns to thirty, and thirty to forty, can I look over my life and see purpose, or is having good intentions that never materialize enough?"

Time passes very quickly, and the time God has given us to appreciate we tend to miss by trying to catch up, or make up for lost time. How can we love the life that God has blessed us with if we use our time doing things that take it away? The time we have in life is not about chasing emotional highs. It is about seeking God and seeing how we can make the biggest spiritual impact possible. Allowing God to use us in a way that elevates the kingdom of God will in turn stabilize us mentally, emotionally, and spiritually.

If this is not what our minds are set on, then any and every little thing will draw us in a direction that can keep us from being about our Father's business in the little time we have here on earth.

The moment our time is up, of course many will say all the right things about us from a moral standpoint. But in our time, did we truly live in the character of Christ? Are the memories we leave behind truly honorable to our Father?

Whether or not we want to look at these truths in-depth, the point is that the answers to these questions do matter. We cannot continue to play with our lives as if time is on our side. Relationships, friendships, marriages, bonds are broken, ill, or never exist, based on our reverence for God and how we utilize our time. We are perfect in Christ — not of ourselves.

We must remain aware of when we make life about ourselves, rather than purpose outside of ourselves. When we do that, we lose track of time. When we do that, love seems to miss us, opportunity seems to pass us, not that it is not there, but we have been so consumed in ourselves that we miss the time to see all that God has promised.

Let's not lose track of time. We must live life with a reverence for God, all while fulfilling our purpose in life. If not, the one thing that is guaranteed in life — death — will seem to come faster than we think. We must urge each other as well as ourselves not to lose track of time.

ASK YOURSELF...

1. As you grow older, does time seem to pass slowly, or does it seem to be speeding up?

2. What can you do today, to make even better use of your limited time?

3. What advice would you give your younger self about using his/her time well?

4. God is infinite. He always was, and He always will be. What does infinity mean to you?

ABOUT JOSHUA PROBY

4,380 days behind bars.
2 years in solitary confinement.
1 life lost.
1 life restored.

Photo by Janella Thaxton

Joshua Proby did not begin to understand his passion for writing until he was in solitary confinement for two years. During that time, the Spirit led him to write. He second-guessed this calling; at the time he could hardly sit still for two minutes, and the notion of sitting down long enough to share even a brief message on his heart seemed laughable — much less the patience to write an entire book.

"Be still and know that I am God."— Psalm 46:10

And so he began to write, despite the negativity that surrounded him when he first put pen to paper.

Joshua still had nine years left on his sentence.

He began to speak to his fellow inmates about the things he had written, too afraid to let anyone read his work for fear of being rejected.

The more he spoke, the more his fellow inmates listened and responded. One particular conversation with a man who was serving a life sentence was a revelation for Joshua. He told the man, "Life is not over." To say that to a man stuck behind bars for life, in Joshua's words, "Is like asking to be shot!" But God protected his life and allowed his words to be seasoned with grace.

And the man asked, "Why do you say that?"

Joshua replied, "When the enemy tries to take a life, God restores life."

Although he couldn't give this man physical freedom, he gave him something even more precious: hope. God used Joshua, behind prison bars, to help others see life in a different way, and to understand that, even behind bars, God has a purpose for each of our lives.

Physical freedom may be gone, but liberty in mind and spirit is priceless — a liberty not many free people truly understand. The walls that hold us hostage take many forms beyond the physical barriers of prison. There are mental prisoners, emotional prisoners, spiritual prisoners — all trapped within themselves.

Joshua's story gives hope to weary souls, and his mission is to share the Good News: Jesus came to set every captive free, and the freedom we seek can be found at the foot of the cross.

Acknowledgements

This book is dedicated to:

My son Jashaun

My daughters, Jeniah, Zavia, and Tynecia

My mother Rhonda

My amazing wife Lecia.

Thank you for supporting me and loving me.

To one of my editors, Elizabeth Sagasar: You took handwriting on prison-issue paper of a young man in solitary confinement and you translated it, helping the message come through. I am forever in your debt.

And to all of the people in and out of prison who've not had the chance to express their pain...

God Bless you all!

---Josh

Made in the USA
Columbia, SC
24 April 2019